MW01602063

Made in United States
Troutdale, OR
02/29/2024

18084773R00067